MW00387285

Only Fools Play Golf in Scotland

in Scotland

And other verses from the gorse

BY

Malcolm MacDougall

Illustrated by Virginia Cantarella

Copyright © 2012 Malcolm MacDougall
All rights reserved. No illustrations in this book may be reproduced, transmitted or stored in a retreval system without the prior written consent of the illustrator, Virginia Cantarella.

Written by Malcolm MacDougall
Illustrated by Virginia Cantarella, Member of the Association of Medical Illustrators and the Graphic Artists Guild
Design by Virginia Cantarella
Copy Editing by Sarah Shonbrun

DEDICATION

Dedicated to David Bentley, Captain of the Green, Patrick McGrath, ACOG, Alan MacDonald, Douglas Johnston, Hugh Walsh and the many other good men who have joined the regulars of The Scottish Golfing Society in our annual rounds of links golf for the past 22 years.

Table of Contents

INTRODUCTION

Most of these verses were hastily scribbled after a humbling day of links golf in Scotland. They were intended to be recited at our long, enthusiastic dinners at Green Craig in Aberlady, Scotland — the official August residence of our very unofficial club, The Scottish Golfing Society.

I believe that my doggerel, like my golf, deserves at least an 18-handicap. Nevertheless, some of the verses seemed to have taken on a life of their own. Several, I am told, have been recited at club dinners and gatherings of golfers in America, Scotland, and Ireland. *The Bunker Hymn of St. Andrews* now has a place of honor at the Royal and Ancient clubhouse. *The Measure of a Golf Hole* appears in Archie Baird's book, "Golf on Gullane Hill." And I'm relieved that *Golfing With the Sheep* did not seem to offend the Board of Directors of Brora when it was recited at their annual dinner.

Now some of my golfing companions have urged me to put them together in book form, and so here they are. I hope you enjoy them. And by the way, you have my permission to recite any of these poems, without accreditation, at any occasion — provided that there are golfers present and wine has been plentifully served.

ONLY FOOLS PLAY GOLF IN SCOTLAND

Only fools play golf in Scotland
Where the wind blows off the Firth
And the cold and rain make golfing
The cruelest sport on earth.

You'll be miserable in Scotland
In those bunkers twelve feet deep
Where you have to hit it backwards
"Cause the bank's too bloody steep."

You've got to be a masochist
To play a Scottish course
Through 18 holes of thrashing
From the heather to the gorse.

I sometimes think the Scots don't know
What golf is all about
For they don't believe in Mulligans
And they make you putt it out.

And in case you still are doubting
That those Scots are silly fools
I must warn you that in Scotland
They make you play the rules.

You may have heard the worst of all
And it isn't idle talk
You won't find any golfing carts —
They actually make you walk!

There are no Scottish country clubs
And that's depressing news.
No swimming pools, no whirlpool baths
And no one shines your shoes!

Those famous links of Scotland
Aren't as great as you've been told.
The rough is badly overgrown
And they're getting rather old.

Carnoustie, Muirfield, Gullane One
They're really all the same.
Their only purpose is to prove
That you can't play this game.

They talk about those frugal Scots
Well here is what they mean -
On the old course at St. Andrews
Two holes must share one green.

The tangled gorse at Dornoch
Is actually said to hide
The bodies of old golfers
Who've committed suicide.

So please don't go to Scotland
Where the wind blows off the firth
And the cold and rain make golfing
The cruelest sport on earth.

Only fools play golf in Scotland
It's not the place to be
So please leave the golf in Scotland
To bloody fools like me.

THE BUNKER HYMN OF ST. ANDREWS

Aye — The Old Course at St. Andrews
Where every bunker is a shrine
I prayed in nearly all of them
As I shot my ninety-nine.

First I visited The Cottage
That caught my drive on four
From there I found The Student's Lair
To exit took two more.

On five I hit a perfect drive
The ball flew straight and true
As I left the tee I felt quite sure
I'd reach the green in two.

But when I reached the fairway
My ball had disappeared
And I heard my caddie chuckle
"Aye — it's just as I had feared."

He led me to a hidden pit
With a monstrous six-foot wall
And pointing to the corner said
"I believe, sir, that's your ball."

Yes, I'd found the Seven Sisters
Those tarts with fiendish holes
Who hide their evil, sluttish charms
Behind the fairway knolls.

With wedge in hand I disappeared
But I couldn't take a stance
So I flailed away and prayed to God
It seemed my only chance.

I swung so hard I wrenched my back
And raised a nasty blister
But to my chagrin I'd put it in
Another bloody sister.

I swung again, it hit the bank
And started rolling free
But before it stopped, it found its way
To the hole of sister three

Again I swung, again the lip
And back it came in four
It took two more ferocious blasts
Before I left that whore.

I par'd the sixth, quite cocky now
I'd escaped those jaws of hell
'Til my approach on number seven found
A monster called *The Shell*.

*The Short Hole Bunke*r soon became
An enemy of mine
And no pit could be more aptly named
Than the *End Hole* trap on nine.

The next three holes were trouble free
I flew the bunkers clean
Bur the old course was just leading me
To disaster at thirteen.

From *Coffin Bunker* to *Cat's Trap*
And from there to *The Lion's Mouth.*
The pin was directly north of me
But to escape I hit it south.

On the long fourteen I flew *The Beardies*
And hit my second well
But the devil made it come to rest
In the bunker known as *Hell.*

On sixteen I hit a wicked hook
Right up *The Principal's Nose*
From there I entered *Deacon Sime*
After two ferocious blows.

Now the great road hole, famed seventeen
Where golfing history's made
"Oh let me be bunker free —
Please dear God!" I prayed.

Now golfers pray and golfers curse
But a golfer never weeps
Yet I broke that strict commandment
In that bunker known as *Cheapes*.

Aye — the old course at St. Andrews
Where every bunker is a shrine
I prayed in nearly all of them
As I shot my ninety-nine.

But 'til I've played life's final shot
The memory will never fade
The Old Course at St. Andrews
The finest round I've ever played.

THE URINAL'S REVENGE

Dedicated to that proud manufacturer,
Armitage Shanks, whose name is emblazoned
on nearly every urinal in Scotland

Let's contemplate that gentleman
Who's earned such sordid fame
That every man in Scotland
Is now pissing on his name.

They say that he's the man who spread
That hideous disease
That's brought the finest golfers
Quivering to their knees.

They say he laid a vengeful curse
On every golfer's game
And thus we have that ghastly shot
That bears his dreaded name.

Your ball is on the fairway
Your swing is smooth and tight
When for no apparent reason
It shoots directly right.

You watch helpless and astounded
As it hurtles off the course
And instead of on the green
You're in Muirfield's deepest gorse.

Now how can I describe
That dreadful sideways shot
That so quickly makes a lovely round
Go utterly to pot?

Well that shot is like a toilet
That some child forgot to flush
It's like a colonoscopy
Or that vile vaginal thrush.

That shot is like that final gasp
As you fall and clutch your heart
That shot is like a loud and noxious
Elevator fart

Yes — this is what he's done to us
I can think of nothing worse
But now the Scots have found a way
To exorcise his curse.

He's caused such devastation
To that noble Scottish game
That every urinal in Scotland
Now bears his evil name.

So to the urinals of Scotland
All golfers owe their thanks
What sweet revenge to piss upon
Old Armitage Shanks.

Armitage Shanks

A FEW THOUGHTS WHILE STANDING
OVER A TWO-FOOT PUTT

Pity that my first putt slipped slightly past the lip
But here I am just two feet away.
I'll just tap the bugger in, give my modest grin
And by George! I'll have carried the day.

But perhaps I should pause for a moment or two
While good old Bentley concedes this wee putt
I mean how could a man who has called me his friend
Conceivably do anything but?

But now look at that bastard — not saying a word
Pretending to stare into space
Well - like a kick in the butt, my little putt
Will wipe that snide smirk off his face!

Yes, I'll feel even better as I watch my ball drop
And I beat that old faggot one-up
I'll just give a little tap, and that will be that
Smack in the back of the cup.

I'm glad it's a putt I can't possibly miss
Just a smooth little two-foot tap.
But perhaps to be sure, instead of a tap
I should give it a good solid rap.

I can see that the putt is perfectly straight
Perhaps the tiniest break to the right
Of course the grain of the green could take the ball left
But that break would be ever so slight.

As I look at it now, it seems slightly uphill
But just a dite downhill at the end
And a bit before the lip, I think I detect
A barely perceptible bend.

Well no need to think — just stand up and putt
I'm quite sure that I've got the right read.
I must simply remember, at the start of my stroke
That the line depends on the speed.

I seem to recall – it was a putt much like this
That Freddy Couples missed on TV
But Couples was careless – he barely took aim
I'm sure it can't happen to me.

Hark! What was that? That dastardly noise?
I could swear I heard Bentley sigh.
That unsportsman-like creep! He can't rattle me
No matter how hard he may try.

But just to be safe, I'll now mark my ball
And repeat my pre-putt routine
I should first check the wind, and the grain of the green
And make sure that my golf ball is clean.

Now let's look at this putt from the other side
For a fresh perspective on this.
Ah! Just as I thought. It's quite a straight putt.
A putt I can't possibly miss.

Well we've covered it all, so let's go back to the ball
Now the moment's upon us to putt.
A smooth practice swing, a glance at the hole,
And for Bentley the door will be shut.

But I must be quite certain to keep my head down
And whatever I do don't look up
'Til the moment I hear that glorious "clank!"
As the ball hits the bottom of the cup.

Now there's nothing to do but to take a deep breath
And make sure that my head doesn't sway
Just two little feet, a smooth easy stroke
And we'll put that old bugger away.

So take a deep breath — and keep the wrists firm
This putt is money in the bank
Just hold the head down and take a smooth stroke
And wait for that marvelous "clank!"

Here we go now — we draw the club back
And take an instant to pray
A firm follow through — and there's no more to do
The ball is now on its way.

(PREGNANT PAUSE)

Twenty-four inches — just two little feet
That's all my ball had to travel
It just goes to show how little it takes
For a good man's life to unravel.

So I think that I'll stand here the rest of my days
And never lift up my head.
For I prayed for the sound of that wonderful "clank!"
But I heard only silence instead.

OLD GOLFERS NEVER DIE

Let young men dream their greedy dreams
Of Lamborghini cars
Of winning fame, becoming rich
And fucking movie stars.

As we grow old, we put aside
Those foolish, childish dreams
And concentrate instead upon
More realistic schemes.

Old golfers have a modest goal
As life turns each new page
While we grow old our only dream
Is just to shoot our age.

Now some might say this lofty goal
Is wishing on a star
For my handicap is now eighteen
And my age is even par.

But consider that I gain a stroke
With every passing year
So as I'm growing older
My goal is drawing near.

If every year I cut one stroke
From my average score
I'll shoot my age at 8I
At worst, at 84.

But let's assume, as years go by
My handicap's the same.
Well, I'll be pushing 90 when
I play that perfect game.

It can be tough to play your best
With two arthritic knees
And I'm sure it's hard to sink a putt
With Parkinson's disease.

So I won't try to push my luck
I must be fair to me
I might not reach my cherished goal
'til I'm a hundred three.

Now my walker might impair my swing
As I try to hit the ball
And it could be hard to keep one's score
With shots one can't recall.

So on second thought, perhaps it's wise
To revise my goal again.
I'm sure that I will shoot my age
When I'm a hundred ten.

But if I fail, and fail again
I'll never rant and rage.
For old golfers never die, my friends
Until they shoot their age.

THE TESTIMONY OF REGINALD SMYTHE

Your honor – I must plead guilty as charged
To what this court has deemed homicide
But I'm sure that you'll find in your wisdom
That my actions were quite justified.

I can assure you that I'm most deeply grieved
That my old friend Bentley is dead
And it's true that I wielded the five iron
Found embedded in poor Bentley's head.

But when you weigh my one burst of temper
Against nine holes of Bentley's abuse
I know you'll agree that my one little act
Has a valid — even noble — excuse.

You should know that he questioned my handicap
As we stood on the very first tee
He said I should play him at twenty
Though he knew I'm a true twenty three.

Thus he began by insulting my honor
Which alone is a dueling offense
I then caught him counting the clubs in my bag
What gentleman would not be incensed?

Now it's tradition that we take a mulligan
A second drive off the opening tee
So imagine my mood when I came to my ball
And he declared I was lying three.

On the next hole he told the tedious joke
That he'd told a good ten times before
And when I declared my six at the end of the hole
He had the nerve to question my score!

On the fourth green Bentley forced me to putt
What a gentleman would naturally concede
When I missed — a slight smirk twitched on his face
A gentleman? This Bentley? Indeed!

Now I didn't get mad when he made his remark
About my pink Brooks Brothers pants
And I held my tongue when he had to bring up
What I'd done at the country club dance.

No, I don't like to cast aspersions upon
A man who has lately departed
But whenever I started my backswing
Bentley deliberately farted!

Yet I managed to keep my composure
Though I was having a rather bad day.
In fact I found myself seven down
After only eight holes of play.

But on the ninth my approach shot was perfect
It stopped three feet from the pin!
"I'm afraid you've hit the wrong ball," he said
While flashing his hideous grin.

The next thing that happened is a bit of a blank
It's something I just don't recall.
It seems that I swung — and hit something hard
That apparently wasn't the ball.

It's quite sad — the demise of poor Bentley
But I'm sure that this merciful court
Will concur in its infinite wisdom
That it was done for the good of the sport.

HOW TO PLAY GOLF

Some instructive thoughts after reading
"The Physics of Golf" by Theodore Jorgensen

You can forget all those costly instructions
And those books on improving your swing.
Until you have learned the science of golf
Those lessons aren't worth a damn thing.

Now that I've studied the physics of golf
And learned professor Jorgensen's tips
I'm really quite sure I can easily cure
Your shanks and your yanks and your yips.

Let's begin with the simplest lesson of all
What to think as you take up your stance.
Just consider the basic Newtonian laws
And you're sure to leave nothing to chance.

As you draw the club back, the linear motion
Is creating centrifugal force.
The angular momentum should position your shoulders
At 90 degrees to the course.

As you rotate your hips, the centripetal thrust
Will generate momentum and torque.
This in turn will begin to uncock your wrists
Like a vintner removing a cork.

While considering that, you must focus your thoughts
On keeping your left arm straight
While the linear pull on your shoulder begins
That crucial shift of your weight.

We now have reached the top of your swing
And you must set your mind on one notion.
Just recite in your head the immutable laws
Of linear and rotational motion.

As the downswing begins and your club head unwinds
There's a small calculation to heed.
The kinetic force of a body in motion
 Will depend on the square of the speed.

Now rotate your hips on a vertical axis
Perpendicular to the plane of your swing
While your arms and your legs, your back and your ass
Do their dynamic energy thing.

If the shift velocity and arc of your swing
Have both been properly reckoned
You can easily compute your club head speed
Up to 200 feet per second.

As the club meets the ball, you must simply consider
The Newtonian law of motion.
The torque from your wrists, plus your angular force
Determine the velocity quotient

Now the physics of golf are immutable laws
That are quite important to know
Though I can't guarantee they'll have any effect
On where the ball may happen to go.

But I hope that this lesson finally proves
The most vital instruction of all.
The way to play golf is to ignore all this crap
Just stand up and hit the damn ball!.

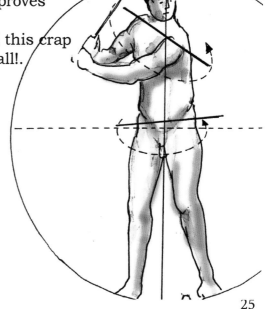

THE MEASURE OF A GOLF HOLE

To judge a man by length alone
Is really rather mean.
So why try to judge a golf hole
By yards from tee to green?

Now the second hole at Gullane One
Is not so very long
But the fool who doubts its manhood
Will be proven very wrong.

The scorecard says 380 yards
A comfortable par 4.
But those yards can be deceiving
As a Piccadilly whore.

It's all uphill from tee to green
This God forsaken place
And no matter how the wind blows
It's always in your face.

The left hand gorse is 3 feet deep
The right is just as mean
But the thing that really gives one pause
There seems nothing in between.

You tee your ball and start to feel
A growing sense of doom
Like entering a graveyard
And your name is on a tomb.

You hit your drive a careful blow
And feel quite safe until —
The wind sweeps off the Firth of Forth
And swoops down for the kill.

It flings your ball to the deepest patch
Of Gullane's primal gorse
As you curse the wretched Scotsman
Who designed this monstrous course.

Not since the march up Bunker Hill
Have bold men fought so hard
Just to conquer one small hill
Yard by bloody yard.

They call this hole the "Windy Gate."
And I think they named it well
For the wind that blows down Gullane Hill
Could part the gates of hell.

Our group of six took on this hole
And when we'd had our licks
The average score of six fine men
Was a humbling 6.6.

It's just a short and scruffy hole
It's not so well endowed
But anyone who makes par here
Should feel forever proud.

For the second hole on Gullane One
Is God's ingenious plan
To prove that length is not the measure
Of a golf hole — or a man.

GOLFING WITH THE SHEEP

You can have your fancy country clubs
That pamper rich old farts
Who drive around their perfect course
In stylish golfing carts.

All their rules and their committees
They can take a flying leap
For I'd rather play at Brora
And go golfing with the sheep.

Yes — high in Northern Scotland
Along the cold North Sea
There's the course that God and nature
Intended golf to be.

The Brora Golf Club has a rule
So dues can't get too steep
They ask that players share their course
With grazing cows and sheep.

It's true your ball may come to rest
On a squishy bovine paddy
But it's not as bad as the shit you take
From some hundred dollar caddy.

You have friendlier companions
When you play with sheep and cows
And they never, ever question
What the R and A allows.

Sheep won't try to fix your swing
Or double-check your score
Or bitch about your handicap
Like some crass old golfing bore.

Now the weather at old Brora
Isn't fit for man or beast
But you're braving it together
There's some comfort there at least.

They placed electric fences
Surrounding every green
You must gingerly step over them
For the shock can be quite mean.

A local rule says fairway turds
May be played as casual water
And with all those gorgeous sheep around
Who needs the farmer's daughter?

When we played the short 14th hole
What a charming sight to see
Ten sheep were munching by the green
And a cow was on the tee.

She watched me as I teed it up
And I thought I hit it true
But as it landed in the bunker
I heard this doleful "Moooo."

No — those stuffy, fancy country clubs
Can take a flying leap
For I'd far rather be at Brora
And go golfing with the sheep.

RULES CONCERNING THE LANGUAGE OF GOLF

Golf is a game that seems to induce
An unfortunate need for profanity
Some golfers maintain that a bellowing curse
Is the means to preserving their sanity.

Even priests have been known, upon missing a putt
To take the Lord's name in vain
And respectable ladies, when fluffing a shot
Use 4-letter words to complain.

So the time has now come for the language of golf
To be governed by logical rules
Words like "Oh, Shit!" must now be replaced
With metaphors such as "Oh, Stools!"

If you're well brought-up, and properly schooled
In a respectable boarding academy
You'll refrain from describing a poor golfing shot
With parts of a woman's anatomy.

When you hit a long putt just a trifle too hard
And it rolls down a slope off the green
You're allowed to utter a colorful curse
But nothing that's truly obscene.

If you've finished a hole and they ask for your score
When you've just shot a dreadful other
Kindly refrain from making it plain
What your opponent can do with his mother.

When you hit a poor drive and it flies out of bounds
Or into the deepest gorse
Please try to confine describing the line
To conventional intercourse.

If you find that your ball's in a devilish bunker
And you need to express your bad luck
On your first blow, say "Damn." On your second say,"Hell."
Please wait 'til the third to say "Fuck!"

Now remember that golf is a gentleman's game
And gentlemen never should curse.
Use an occasional "Shit," or an appropriate "Fuck."
But please refrain from anything worse.

HUGS' HILL

A Petition to the Board of Governors of The Gullane Golf Club
Respectfully Submitted by The Scottish Golfing Society

Gentlemen*:*

We propose that you place an appropriate plaque
On the crest of Gullane 2
To honor a feat as heroic as any
On Everest of Katmandu.

For today Hugs Walsh reached the top of hole 3
And he did it without pitons or pick.
He made the ascent with a caddy as Sherpa
And the support of a golfing stick.

Now we presume you'll insist that he wasn't the first
For it's only a simple par 4.
But we assure you the climb has never been made
By a golfer like Hugs before.

Here is a man who was one step from death
Back in August of 2001.
He had attempted to challenge this monstrous hill
And the hill had resoundingly won.

Undaunted, our hero returned to the scene
In late August of 2005.
Determined to prove that he still had the grit
To conquer the summit alive.

In spite of his lungs that make each breath he takes
A gasping, asthmatic wheeze;
In spite of arthritis, lumbago and gout,
And a liver like limburger cheese.

In spite of his knees that buckle at will
And a body so far past its prime.
In spite of the excess weight he must carry
Plucky Hugs began the long climb.

Upwards! Upwards! Bravely Upwards!
His visage contorted with pain
Stoically pausing to hit the white ball
Which he did — again and again

At last at the summit a grey head appeared
Then a deathly, ashen face.
His devoted friend Bentley tried to give the Last Rights
But he only knew how to say Grace.

Just as we thought he'd drawn his last breath
Miraculously, Hugs revived.
In spite of all odds, the summit was won
And Excelsior! Hugs survived!

So we propose that you place an appropriate plaque
To honor his indomitable will.
The inscription should state that this hallowed ground
Will forever be known as "Hugs' Hill."

UPON ASKING A SCOTSMAN
"WHAT'S THE BEST COURSE IN GULLANE?"

"So laddie — you want me to tell you
the best course in Gillin, eh?
Well that's not so easy to say.

"I suppose it depends on
what kind of golfer you are,
and how you happen to play.

"Now back there is Muirfield.
A real gentlemen's club,
And a true devil of a course.

"You'll find bunkers as deep
as the craters of hell, and
you'll be up to your ass in gorse.

"Aye, but you'd be hard put to find
a truer test of golf.
And that's the bloody sin.

"'Cause if you're not a member
or the fookin' Duke of Marlborough
you nae have a chance to get in.

"Now if you'll look way over there
you'll see one of our oldest courses.
It happens to be called Luffness New.

"It'll give you a lively round alright.
But the rough's so thick you'll lose
a dozen balls before you're through.

"Now, you want a real challenge, do ya?
And you think steep hills, stiff winds
and long, tough holes are fun.

"Well look up at the hill over there.
That's a real golf course, laddie.
Aye — that's our Gillin One.

Some say it's the finest course in Scotland.
But look out when the wind's up
For the ball never goes where it should.

"One day you'll take a wedge to the green.
The next day you can't get there
with your longest fairway wood.

"You'll have lovely green fairways
And mighty fine views.
But the rough's getting a bit tall.

"You could hide a body in there
and you're no more likely to find it
than you can find your fookin' ball.

"Now over there's a slightly gentler course,
but a true challenge nevertheless.
It's our lovely Gillin Two.

"And if you're strong enough to make it
to the top of the third hole
Ah — you'll have a glorious view!

"Now down the road apiece is our newest course
It's called Craigelaw, and oh it can be a monster
when the weather's raw and windy.

"And right next door, hard against the Firth
 is our gentle lamb that's been there forever.
It's our grand old Kilspindie.

"But if you've nae played in Scotland afor
I think the best game for you would be
To play a round over there — on Gillin Three.

"It's a kindly course, and it just so happens
right now myself,
I'm on my way to the tee.

"The fact is, laddie, if you love the game of golf
the seven courses of Gillin
are all about the same.

"And in fact I'd be honored if you'd just
park your car over there
And join me in a wee little game."

ODE TO SPOTTED DICK
(Or getting your just desserts of Muirfield)

Lord Nelson craved his Spotted Dick
And Lady Nelson, too.
Wellington had Spotted Dick
After Waterloo.

Three centuries of royalty
Have relished Spotted Dick.
They say that Queen Victoria
Liked hers extra thick.

Now thanks to Muirfield's kindly hosts
I'm rather pleased to say
The Spotted Dick tradition
Is alive and well today.

They'll gladly serve you Spotted Dick
Plus after-luncheon drinks
But first you'll have to earn your Dick
On Muirfield's mighty links.

You'll have to stand on that first tee
A weak and frightened thing
While the Gods of Golf are laughing
At your less than perfect swing.

You'll have to walk where Vardon walked
On this hallowed course
Knowing he strolled down the fairway
While you're thrashing through the gorse.

You'll have to play the frightful fifth
The hole that champions curse
And fear that waiting just ahead
Is something even worse.

For then you'll play the nasty sixth
And there you'll find your ball
Buried in the tangled rough
Behind an ancient wall.

You'll have to take your lumps again
On dreaded number nine
And still you've got nine more to go
Before they'll let you dine.

You'll have to try to exit from
That bunker on thirteen
A nasty pit that's deep enough
To hide a submarine.

You'll have to thrash through buckthorn
That stretches to the green
And then you must negotiate
That endless seventeen.

And when you reach that 18th green
You'll hang your head in shame
As members in the club house watch —
And comment on your game

Yes you'll have to pay for luncheon
On Muirfield's fabled course
Where the price of great rice pudding
Is 18 holes of gorse.

But once you've had a Scotch or two
And roast beef red and thick
By God — you'll get your just desserts
You've earned your Spotted Dick.

GOLF IS A THINKING GAME

When a pitcher throws a baseball
At 90 miles an hour
You simply try to hit the ball
With pure, unthinking power.

When you race to catch a football
You don't pause to look around
You just know that when you catch it
You'll be hammered to the ground.

When you're at the net in tennis
There's never time to think
"Cause the ball will whiz right past you
If you so much as blink.

But golf's a different kind of game
A game that makes you think
Which is why we have the 19th hole
To drown our thoughts in drink.

There's so much stuff to think about
Before you hit the ball
I think it's quite astounding that
We hit the ball at all.

You have to think about your backswing
And how to follow through
You have to think about the people that
You think are watching you.

You have to think about your posture.
You have to think about your stance.
You have to think about how good you look
In your pink Nantucket pants.

You have to think about your elbow.
You have to think about your knee.
You have to think about how far you'll walk
Before you get to pee.

You have to think about what club to use
And the distance to the pin.
You have to think about the texture
Of the bloody rough you're in.

You have to think about that lesson
On how to cure your slice.
You have to think about your partner's
Latest bad advice.

You have to think about the times
When you hit the ball so well.
You have to think about the punch line
Of the joke you want to tell.

You've got so much to think about
When you're finally on the green
You begin to think your head's become
A damn computer screen.

I wish that I could just forget
What every pro has said
And figure out a simple way
To empty out my head.

For if only I could play the game
With nothing on my mind
I know I'd play at even par
Instead of ninety-nine.

I think that I could give it up
And hang my head in shame
If I didn't think that someday
I could beat this thinking game.

THE WINDS OF NORTH BERWICK

If golf was meant to punish you
For all your earthly sins
Then you should play North Berwick West
In Scotland's blustery winds.

Oh, you're sure to get religion
When you go golfing there
For every time you hit the ball
You say a silent prayer.

But it's kind of hard to worship
These hallowed golfing grounds
When the first drive that you hit here
Goes sailing out of bounds.

And you won't enjoy the scenery
On that lovely second tee
When the wind lifts your golf ball
And sends it out to sea.

On the third you think you've crushed the ball
Unleashing all your power
But the wind just sends it back to you
At 40 miles an hour

Now the fourth is just a simple hole
A short, downhill par three
But when the wind is up you'd better use
A driver off the tee.

The wind will take your golf ball
To the bunkers and the gorse
It just makes sure you never play
The fairway on the course.

The first nine is your penance
For straying from God's path
So every time you hit the ball
You'll feel His awful wrath.

You bow your head and buck the wind
And plead you've had enough
Then pray that you can find your ball
In North Berwick's ghastly rough.

Yes, golf was meant to punish you
For all your earthly sins
But you can find forgiveness
When the final nine begins.

For you suddenly discover that
Your torture has an end
As North Berwick's howling gale
Becomes your golfing friend.

Now the wind just lifts your ball
And flies it straight and far
And instead of triple bogeys
You now are shooting par.

The Twelfth's a bird, the Pit's a par
You're perfect on Perfection
And the way you play the famed Redan
Could cause a slight erection.

And when at last you hit your drive
On the short par 4 eighteen
The wind will gently take your ball
And place it on the green.

Yes, golf was meant to punish you
For all your greed and sins
And you'll be truly punished
In North Berwick's mighty winds.

But you'll also find redemption
And you'll never feel remorse
For you've had the joy of playing golf
On God's favorite Scottish course.

WHEN REGINALD SMYTHE PLAYED
THE GAME OF HIS LIFE

It was a beautiful evening at North Berwick West
Not a breath of wind in the air.
Old Reginald Smyth had to play by himself
What a pity no members were there.

For he birdied the first with a magnificent wedge
That nearly went into the hole.
He made par on the second with a 30-foot putt
That took a most favorable roll.

His drive on the fourth caught the bank on the right
And funneled quite close to the pin.
He looked all about — hoping someone would see
As his three-foot putt dropped in.

Now Reginald had talked about shooting his age
Ever since he turned eighty-two
But sadly a 90 one day at Kilspindie
Was the best he'd been able to do.

But that evening he somehow discovered his game
His drives would fly long and straight
And old Reginald was still at one over par
When he stood on the tee at eight.

Now eight is a long and nasty par five
And he'd never shot better than six
But he easily made par for this was a round
When magically everything clicks.

His drive on the ninth was a wonder to see
He'd never hit a ball half as far
A smooth three-wood, and a lovely approach
And by God! Two putts and a par!

He played the back nine as though in a trance
He chipped-in for par at eleven
He parred hole after hole — yes, even the Redan
Every swing seemed directed from heaven.

His drive on eighteen ended close to the green.
Oh what a pity that no one was there.
For when he chipped the ball close and sank the next putt
His joy was mixed with despair.

After his round he pinched himself twice
To see if he was really alive
For Reginald Smyth, believe it or not
Had shot a seventy-five.

He rushed to the club, to announce the good news
But the manager was locking the door.
He responded with a smile and a sarcastic chuckle
When Reginald shouted his score .

Later that night he was feeling quite dazed
As he sat all alone at the pub
Where he wrote a long note describing his round
And sent it on to the club.

"As God is my witness," Reginald wrote
"Though this may be a shock to you
This evening I shot a seventy-five
I swear on my honor it's true."

Now he knew it would never get better than this
For he'd just shot the round of his life
But those bastards will never believe me, he thought
Nor will my cynical wife.

The next day they found him, stone cold dead
A bullet lodged in his brain.
Based on the score card clutched in his hand
The coroner declared him insane.

At the club they agreed that he'd quite lost his mind
And his death was all for the best
For they all had read that ridiculous note
That he'd sent to North Berwick West.

Now the moral of Reginald is really quite clear
And it ought to be etched in stone.
Someday you might play the round of your life
So you never should play golf alone!

| COMPETITION R.SMYTHE | | | | DATE | | Handicap | Stroke |

Hole	Name	White Yards	Blue Yards	Par	Stroke Index	A	B
1	Point Garry (out)	323	308	4	9	3	
2	Sea	432	418	4	11	4	
3	Trap	460	444	4	1	5	
4	Carlekemp	178	168	3	15	2	
5	Bunkershill	370	358	4	5	5	
6	Quarry	160	139	3	17	4	
7		354	334	4	3	4	
8	Linkhouse	506	487	5	13	5	
9	Mizzentop	520	502	5	7	6	
OUT		3303	3158	36		37	
10	Eastward Ho!	171	152	3	18	4	
11	Bos'ns Locker	548	524	5	2	5	
12	Bass	397	362	4	8	4	
13	Pit	388	362	4	12	5	
14		376	359	4	6	4	
15	Redan	190	179	3	14	3	
16	Gate	379	349	4	4	5	
17	Point Garry (in)	428	385	4	10	3	
18	Home	278	271	4	16	3	
IN		3155	2943	35		38	
OUT		3303	3158	36		37	
TOTAL		6458	6101	71		75	

Handicap   Nett

YIPS

Don't speak to me of pleurisy
Or ghastly anal drips
You just don't know what suffering is
Until you've had The Yips.

The Yips can make the strongest man
A quivering helpless wraith
The Yips can make a pious priest
Renounce the Catholic faith.

I've had The Yips, and now I know
What true neurosis means
It's the tragic nervous breakdown that
Occurs on putting greens.

Your mind is overtaken with
A creeping cowardice
You tremble over every putt
Convinced you're going to miss.

Your innards tighten up in knots
Your fingers turn to stone
You lose all sense of confidence
You've no testosterone.

You'd rather be on life support
Or floundering in the gutter
Than put your trembling hands around
Your sick, contagious putter.

Your head begins to vibrate and
Your body starts to shimmy
When opponents start to smell your fear
There's no such thing as "gimme."

I've consulted several doctors
And heard a hundred tips
But there isn't any simple cure
For that vile disease — The Yips.

But if they can make a pill that helps
Old fogies get it up
Why can't they make a pill that helps
Us sink a two-foot putt?

So don't talk to me of dysentery
Or disgusting anal drips
No sickness is more ghastly than
That vile disease The Yips.

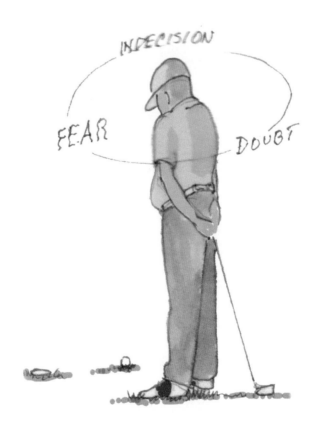

THE BALLAD OF THE DREADED OTHER

Oh we dance like the monkey on a hurdy-gurdy
When our approach hits the green — and we sink it for birdie!
And I know when we write our golfing memoirs
We'll describe at great length every one of our pars.

We're hardly discouraged when we wind up with bogies
For that's par for the course for us certified fogies.
And because there are times when we do find some trouble
We can even feel proud when we rescue a double.

If a triple should happen — well it's just rotten luck.
We're allowed to say "Shit!" Or murmur a "Fuck."
Quadruple is messy. Quintuple's quite bad.
But in truth it's a score that everyone's had.

But now let's consider that ultimate shame
The score that could make us give up the game.
It's a hole that could drive us to curse our dear Mother.
I'm referring, of course, to - that Dreaded Other.

It starts with a slice that just makes the rough
And your second winds up in some nastier stuff.
You then hit a "flier" that flies out of bounds
While your stomach starts making loud gurgling sounds.

Your fifth is hit well, but it catches a tree
And you break your six iron over your knee.
The next is a rather unfortunate try
To play a clearly unplayable lie.

Your face has turned red, your eyes are rolled back
You're sure that you're suffering a heart attack.
But somehow you stoically stifle a cry.
You're determined to hole out before you die.

Your golfing companions are now far ahead
And you fervently pray that all three will drop dead.
Just look at them smirking and telling their jokes.
You can tell that the bastards are counting your strokes.

There's a bush and a creek and a shank in between
And three blasts from the bunker just off the green.
Then a putt and another, and another and another
And finally you've finished that Dreaded Other.

Now when golf was invented, there wasn't a plan
To let one little hole destroy a good man.
Golf should be fun, it's a game that depends
On having some laughs and making good friends.

That's why we give mulligans on the first tee
And why many a putt's been conceded to me.
So I hereby propose that we love one another
And simply not count that Dreaded Other.

THE JOY OF ALZHEIMER'S GOLF

I recall that drive I hit on five
I still see its soaring flight,
Its graceful arc, its mighty thrust
Not veering left or right.

I can see it now, that mighty drive
That flew so straight and true
It went 30 yards past Bentley's ball
And I said "old friend — screw you!"

I recall that downhill 12-foot putt
That I struck so well on ten.
I still see it gently rolling right,
Then swerving left again.

I shan't forget that perfect putt,
That slow, deliberate roll,
Or that look on old Bentley's face
As it dropped into the hole.

And I recall that lovely lob
That I struck on seventeen
That flew high above the bunker
Landing softly on the green.

It rolled across that tricky green
Stopping two feet from the pin.
I won't forget that surge of joy
As I proudly stroked it in.

I remember well those lovely shots
And I'd love to tell you more
But I simply can't remember
Those other ninety four.

But that's the joy of playing golf
When you're old as me.
I remember all the good shots
And forget the misery.

"IF ONLY" — A GOLFER'S LAMENT

If there were any justice in this merciless game of golf
I'd gladly play my game without complaint.
But the fate that follows me from the first bloody tee
Would surely try the patience of a saint.

If my lovely opening drive hadn't hit that hidden mound
It never would have wound up in the bunker.
And if that spike mark hadn't pushed my perfect bogey putt
There can't be any doubt that I'd have of sunk her.

If they'd put the stakes in properly on that tricky number four
They could never rule my ball was out of bounds.
And on five I would have sunk that simple two-foot putt
If Bentley hadn't made those farting sounds.

If the wind hadn't gusted as I hit on number six
I would easily have cleared that stupid tree.
If the fool who built this course had an ounce of common sense
He'd know that tree is where a tree should never be.

If my caddy had the brains to watch the bloody ball
I wouldn't have had to hit again on nine.
And if that arrogant MacDonald hadn't called that stupid rule
Well — I still maintain the ball I hit was mine.

I could have shot an 80 — or at worst an 82
If the Scots weren't too cheap to mow the rough.
And I would have had a four — not that fucking eight
If my drive on twelve had missed that prickly stuff.

We should have won the match without the shadow of a doubt
If McGrath had only played a little better
And if he hadn't muttered "oops" every time I hit the ball
And if he hadn't worn that ghastly tartan sweater.

If there were the slightest bit of justice in this bloody game of golf
I would graciously accept my golfing fate.
But where's the God damn justice — when I could have shot an 80
Yet my score card shows this ghastly 98.

A PRAYER FOR OUR BALLS

God has heard our tearful curses
Our anguished caterwauls
But now it's time to sanctify
Our poor, beloved balls.

So I ask you all to bow your heads
And say a silent prayer
For all our balls that went astray
And now lie God knows where.

Let us pray for the balls that were gone with the wind
And those that were lost at sea.
Let us pray for those lovely virgin balls
That went astray off the very first tee.

Let us pray for the balls that flew out of sight
And lie buried in North Berwick West.
May the tangle of grass that serves as their shroud
Preserve their eternal rest.

Let us pray for the balls that disappeared
Into Muirfield's deepest rough.
Let us pray for the balls now buried deep
In Carnoustie's ghastly stuff.

Let us pray for the balls in thistles and creeks
That never will be found.
Especially those now enshrined forever
In St. Andrew's hallowed ground.

Let us pray for the balls on Gullane One
Entombed in gorse and heather.
I know several I hit on the second hole
Now lie buried there together.

Pray forgive us sinners who went astray
And missed our Sunday church
And instead went tramping through the rough
In our endless golf ball search.

And let us pray we never try to add
How much those lost balls cost.
Above all pray we never count
All the freaking strokes we lost.

THE ONLY CURE FOR AWFUL GOLF

How can you soothe the shattered mind
Of a poor tormented soul
Whose drives can't find the fairways
Whose putts can't find the hole.

What can you do when a good friend's game
Is so impossible to fix
That he shoots a 107
Where he once shot 76.

How can you help a once proud man
Who is sound in body ... but
Is physically unable
To sink a simple two-foot putt.

How can you save a golfer
Whose natural, fluid swing
Has suddenly become
A flailing spastic thing.

What can you say to a golfing chum
Whose game has sunk so low
That you wince and hide your head
At his every feeble blow.

Now we all know shallow sympathy
Can't help these tortured men
And if you try to make a joke of it
They'll never play again.

Now some may turn to God
And devote their lives to prayer
But when they try to play again
Their God is never there.

They should turn instead to science
Where I'm sure a cure they'll find.
A merciful lobotomy
Could do wonders for their mind.

But when their awful yips and shanks
Are too painful to endure
Perhaps a quiet suicide
Might be the simplest cure.

For life has many tragedies
That all of us must face
But a humiliating golf game
Is the ultimate disgrace.

So when your game's a shambles
The best advice for you.
Admit your game has gone to hell
Then plan to go there too.

THE DEVILISH GAME

"Oh golf is such a devilish game"
New golfers often say
Not knowing that there really is
An evil force at play.

But we who understand the game
Know this frightening fact:
The Scotsman who invented golf
Had made the Devil's pact.

For we have heard that demon voice
That crawls inside our head
And says "Forget that easy swing
Hit hard and fast instead."

A par 5 hole — we drive it well
And a nice lay-up will do
But that soft satanic voice insists
"Let's go for it in two."

So we take our trusty three-wood
And give a mighty smash.
Then hear that fiendish laughter
And an awful, distant splash.

When our ball is nestled in the woods
That voice is loud and clear
"Just hit it low between those trees
You've not a thing to fear."

Your partner pleads, "Just pitch it out
And settle for your bogey."
But that voice says "Play it like a man.
Not some quivering old fogey."

When your partner shakes his head and says
"This time you really blew it."
It's embarrassing to have to say
"The Devil made me do it."

No, the Devil's there on every shot
No point in getting pissed
How else could any one explain
Those two-foot putts you missed?

And only fools could fail to see
That crafty Devil's hand
When your ball is in the bunker
Half buried in the sand.

When you make a lovely, perfect swing
Yet get a dreadful shank
You know who's up to his old tricks
Yes — you know just who to thank.

You can rant and curse for all you're worth
But down deep you know damn well
It doesn't help to tell the devil
"You can go to hell!"

If your average score is 81
But you shoot a hundred two
You can be quite sure old Lucifer
Is really pissed at you.

If you wonder why the more you play
Your score keeps getting worse
It's because your one true handicap
Is that dark Satanic curse.

So remember when you pony up
At the end of a losing day
You'd better pay the Devil
Or there'll be Hell to pay

For it's true that golf's a devilish game
It's never on the level
You may win a friendly game or two
But you'll never beat the Devil.

A PLEA FOR THE DEFENSE
IN THE MATTER OF THE BUNKER RAKES

With permission, your Honor, I'd like to explain
The event that occurred August 10
At the meeting of our club's Golfing Committee
Who are all most honorable men.

The Committee had before it some critical matters
They had met until quite late at night
And earlier they'd dined with considerable wine
Which might explain the unfortunate fight.

They'd discussed club matters of vital concern
Which they calmly debated for hours
Such as the crest for the caps of the caddies
And the proper soap for the ladies' showers.

It was the last item on the evening's agenda —
The placement of the bunker rakes.
And I trust that your Honor can appreciate
What a critical difference this makes.

Mr. Bentley proposed that the club make a rule
That all rakes must be placed in the sand
Thus rendering them less likely to interfere
With the way a golf ball might land.

But then Mr. Ryder quite strongly declared
"The rakes should be left on the grass!"
Mr. Bentley who's a bit hard of hearing
Thought Mr. Ryder had called him an "ass."

Mr. Roski then tried to calm their discussion
By offering another suggestion.
Half in and half out of the bunkers
Was his solution to this delicate question.

Mr. Ryder agreed and he most firmly stated
"Now that's a very good rule."
With that Mr. Bentley rose from his chair
And said, "No one can call me a fool!"

Your Honor it is clear the ensuing assault
Was not done with malicious intent
So I move that this case be summarily dismissed
With your Honor's most gracious consent.

Please consider that old Mr. Bentley
Is a man of considerable standing
And his vicious attack was just the result
Of an unfortunate misunderstanding.

I can assure your Honor the Committee will abide
By whatever decision you make
But may we suggest that this court also determine
Where we should place the damn bunker rake.

ODE TO ABERLADY

About 20 miles from Edinburgh
When you're heading North
You'll come to gentle Aberlady
On the Firth of Forth.

You really ought to go there
So you'll have a chance to see
How life in our too-hectic world
Was really meant to be.

It's just a tiny village
Takes a minute to drive through
But you'll find that fleeting minute
Will always stay with you.

Now modest Aberlady
Has no special claim to fame
It's just a peaceful village
That's as lovely as its name.

Oh the people here have fought their wars
And shared their joys and tears
But the village hasn't changed that much
In the last 900 years.

Aberlady is a tidy town
As clean as Scottish air
A town that seems to whisper —
That you'd be happy there.

A hundred modest cottages
Built of noble stone
That speak of Scottish character
That's solid to the bone.

There's a store where people buy their needs
And a pub to down their beers
They've worshipped in the same stone church
For at least a thousand years.

Folks here tend their gardens
And hope things stay the same.
It's a place that's made for golfers
Who respect the ancient game.

There are 20 nearby courses
The citizens can play
When they're not out watching birds
Over Aberlady Bay.

So here's to Aberlady
A town that has no peers.
May it never change a bit
For another thousand years.

Now if this is sacrilegious
I pray that you'll forgive
But I think if God had a choice
Aberlady's where He'd live.

A PERFECT DAY IN SCOTLAND

The sun shone bright that Sunday
On a perfect August day
The wind was but a whisper
And the clouds had gone away.

The flowers preened their glory
The sky a vibrant blue
From the garden steps of Green Craig
I had a lovely view.

I could see the seagulls soaring
Above the Firth of Forth
And behold a sweeping vista
East, West, South and North.

I could almost see St. Andrews
In the lovely Kingdom Fife
On such a day a man could feel
He lived the perfect life.

Then off we went to Dunbar
My spirits bright and gay
Who could help but play a perfect round
On such a lovely day.

Yes, this is what I'd waited for
The perfect day for par
No wind to toss my ball about
Just hit it straight — and far.

I took my stance and hit my drive
And watched a soaring slice
And suddenly that perfect day
Didn't seem so nice.

Now golf is not a perfect game
You shouldn't rant and curse
Just because — hole by hole —
You go from bad to worse.

And you shouldn't spoil a perfect day
By weeping in the bar
Just because for 18 holes
You were 20 over par.

Yet I was sorely tempted
To slit my wrists and die
For this bloody perfect day meant
I had no alibi.

I can do without a cloudless sky
And the sunshine altogether
For a perfect day in Scotland
Is not about the weather.

Now the sun may shine in paradise
Where every day's the same
But a perfect day in Scotland
Means how well you played the game.

So you can have that bloody sunshine
And the views of Kingdom Fife
For that perfect day in Scotland
Was the worst day of my life.

THE POOR LOST SOULS OF GOLF
(*An ode to Green Craig, home of the Scottish Golfing Society*)

Proud Green Craig on the Firth of Forth
God bless it if you please
For here's a home for those who have
A sad and strange disease.

Folks doff their caps as they walk by
And keep their voices soft
In deference to the Scottish home
For the Poor Lost Souls of Golf.

We all know those who've gone astray
And drowned themselves in drinks
But the Poor Lost Souls of Golf
Are addicted to the links.

The drunks who go to Betty Ford
Get sober, clean and pure
But for Green Craig's golf-aholics
There'll never be a cure.

They've abandoned home and children
And a devastated wife
For they've come to feel the game of golf
Is all there is to life.

Yes, golf is their religion
And they brook no compromise
For all they know of love and life
Is — play it as it lies.

They'd gladly spend a fortune
Without the least regret
Hoping they could beat a friend
On one two-dollar bet.

They pilgrimage to Scotland
Just as often as they can
To pay homage to the courses
Where the noble game began.

It doesn't really matter
How good or bad they play
So long as these poor lost souls
Play eighteen holes a day.

Muirfield, Gullane and old Dunbar
And proud North Berwick West
Until they've played life's final round
The Poor Lost Souls won't rest.

If you joined these souls for dinner
You'd wish that you had not
For you'd have to sit and listen
While they re-played every shot.

They may grow old but they refuse
To leave this earthly strife
Until they've conquered every course
In Lothian and Fife.

And when they die their heirs will find
Directions in their will
To be buried near the 7th hole
On top of Gullane hill.

They all come home to Green Craig
No matter where they've been
For it's the only place in Scotland
That would deign to let them in.

No inn would take these derelicts
The church would chase them off
Only Green Craig has a welcome for
The Poor Lost Souls of Golf.

McGRATH'S MYSTERIOUS PUTT

A golfer who relies upon
Some supernatural force
Should instantly and permanently
Be banished from the course.

So I ask you now to judge
Without prejudice or wrath
If the Devil played a part
In the putt by Pat McGrath.

Pat was off the green
The pin so far away
If he got it down in three
I'd congratulate his play.

The putt was all uphill
For at least 200 feet
With more twists and turns and dips
Than a San Francisco street.

But Patrick took a mighty swing
And the ball was running fast
I gave a knowing smile
As it rolled twelve feet past.

For now he had a downhill putt
Snaking to his right
A putt that Patrick couldn't sink
If he practiced day and night.

But then I noticed Patrick
Staring at his ball
His eyes gave out a reddish glow
Quite weird, as I recall.

Two seconds past, the ball stayed still
Clearly it was dead
But Pat kept up his eerie stare
Then strangely bobbed his head.

There are witnesses to testify
About what happened next
And we all will swear on bibles
That golf ball had been hexed.

For the ball began to tremble
As though wakened from the dead
By some supernatural laser
That had come from Patrick's head.

We watched in eerie silence
As the ball began to move
Slowly, slowly it crept down
Some predetermined groove.

It trickled left. It trickled right.
A demon ball possessed.
I sensed that we'd see evil
When it finally came to rest.

We could only watch in horror
As it neared its hellish goal
And I swear I heard a fiendish laugh
As it dropped inside the hole.

Now I don't mind when Pat McGrath
Sinks an honest putt
And then strides across the green
With his glib, obnoxious strut.

For I know that I can beat McGrath
When I play him on the level
But I have to say to hell with him
When he partners with the Devil.

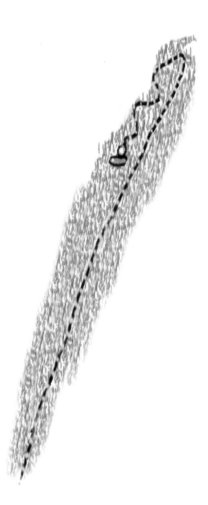

NO ARCHITECT COULD IMITATE
NORTH BERWICK WEST

Most every course we play at home
Claims to have a test
That's sort of like a hole or two
At old North Berwick West.

They'll say they have a little brook
Just like the seventh burn
Or a devastating 5-3-5
Like Berwick at the turn.

They try to make a tough par 5
Like the great eleventh hole
But no one's come within a mile
Of accomplishing that goal.

Most everyone who builds a course
Tries to copy the Redan
Though they know down deep they never will
For no one ever can.

These old stone walls and humpback greens
Along the windswept Firth
They'll never match North Berwick West
Though they try for all they're worth.

No architect could re-create
These subtle dips and rolls
No country club could duplicate
These perfect 18 holes.

They've tried to copy this old course
For 200 years or so
But forgery can't re-create
This Michelangelo.

So let them copy hole by hole
Let them try their best
They soon will learn that only God
Could make North Berwick West.

THE OLD FARTS OF GOLF

You can cheer all you want for those young football stars
But how quickly their glory is gone
Long after they've hung up their tired old jocks
The old farts of golf still play on.

Yes the world should applaud the old farts of golf
The sick, the halt and the lame
As we limp 'round the course and play through our pain
We bring honor and pride to the game.

You should never belittle we geezers of golf
Our wrinkles are the badge of our pride
Our looks are deceiving, opponents be warned
We've the fire of the Tiger inside.

I feel that the records of golf should include
A special curmudgeon page
To celebrate golfers aged 80 or more
Who win the honor of shooting their age.

So let's all raise a glass to the old farts of golf
May our love of the game always thrive
We may be old farts — but there's golf in our hearts
And we know that's what keeps us alive!

6667585R00042

Made in the USA
San Bernardino, CA
12 December 2013